WAVERING KNOTS

A Story Through Poetry

Gladys Marie B. Cubias

RESOURCE *Publications* · Eugene, Oregon

WAVERING KNOTS
A Story Through Poetry

Resource Publications
An Imprint of Wipf and Stock Publishers
199 W. 8th Ave., Suite 3
Eugene, OR 97401

www.wipfandstock.com

PAPERBACK ISBN: 978-1-6667-6706-3
HARDCOVER ISBN: 978-1-6667-6707-0
EBOOK ISBN: 978-1-6667-6708-7

02/07/23

Contents

— Part I —

Oasis

Progressions and evolutions of the minutia

Carousing through bends and thickets of the suburbia

And when the ridges of the hills and the solemn tides ashore
    transform the fiasco

Going towards the light beams coruscated its frightful nature

Vast and untouched, undulated by the gasping air

In an atmospheric height of pressure, breathing leaves
    sheathed through

Flying high above the sprawling yet wonderful oasis
    —in intensity, it flares

And there I can see across the auspicious rays
    of little droplets of depth

Substantiated by insatiable flares and corrosive cries
    —ultimately bare

Balances and stabilities,

Over small and huge propensities

Just right over there, across this edge, life begins.

Beautifully Tarnished

Extraordinarily magnificent but cursed
Like a walking pile of gold over calloused stems of hard roots
Fervid and impeccable halo-like incandescence
But of dragged iron-wrought gait and dense.

Shapely frames bellow the winds,
and caressing the bending unruly willows
hampered touches in ivies and daisies like relentless thorns
scrape like misfortunes of forlorn.
And succumbing to pretty sheaths on leaves of dark and gray,
Presence of stones on foot lands, to say
Oh, beautifully tarnished
—yet grand in a way.

Cinematic Dash

Before my upright vision flashes all these blocks
of paneled tapes, right in delirious frames
while quickly it has commenced
life in cinematic dashes
my sensory has optimistically brazen.

Piece by piece, all strewn to comprehend
the abhorring complexities,
the fastidious creativities,
and hampered particularities,
Dragged for wavering tenacity.

Start The Day With Oranges and Lemons

Freshly pulped, mushy orange flakes
Styled to elegantly drape by the glass of perfection
Varied colors of light and dark,
of opacity and translucence
—is a nice touch to good morning breaks.

You know when it is served
There is pervading glow of sunshine and daze
To quench in flavors of new todays
Pressed to release a tender sensation.

And by the side sits the lemons to complement
The brightness it offers the vintage tables so austerely
A morning feast of exciting todays; quite seemingly
Symbolic of commencing huge propensities
For steps ahead
—across an array of realistic densities

The Train Station

Once I stood by the end of the train station,
pondering about the next hour
To proceed to the elevated steps and hang onto forever
Or to shrink back quite exhaustingly, for yet another time.

Two scenarios—my mind dabbles in a mosaic of possibilities
Caustically dreaming an array of unhinged realities
Or clinging on to high flown strings of reasonings
Next hours flew by quickly—still at the train station

Sat by the crestfallen bench, it seemed like it knew the vibe
To wait a little longer until it becomes liberating
Or to gallop on to the steps—still quite unsure
In several rotes my mind spun, my chest heaves—undecided
    for long

And here comes the last flight for today,
Sprang up from my seat and skedaddled my way through
    the crowd
Towards the line that crosses the boundaries
Took a leap for the uncertain
A desire for the insatiable unknown.

Decadent

26th, decades long gone

Hollow, vast, stares from afar

Daydreaming on nights deliberately undone,

Like floating above tidal waters- unusually calm

Endless chasms, I feel the deep cold rush,

Like a raven flapping in a deafening hush,

"It's time to grow up"- they said

"Time to get real" words propelled

Treaded through ripple tides, I've commenced.

Yet in the process- scared and impaired,

I have fetched and fairly grasped

That in solitude brews a tender good life, and being a kid
    does not worry me quite

Here, still continuously chasing wonderful river tides

In Search Of Wonder

Is happiness what I am trying to reach?
Or sheer comfort in hazy and dreary dreams?
Is smiling all ears worth the chase- in careful majestic haste?
Sometimes, I wonder if the sun still shines on dry roots;
If grass still grows on fields anew;
If water remains crystal and sparkly and never dries up;
Because life moves in directions so foreign;
often enamored by fantasy, but blinded by the uncertain.
Treading pathways with wavering cobblestones;
Slowly and wobbly and sure to fall
Just as unclear and hazy and cloudy and dull—in pedestals
    of stars, in major glimpse
Towards a pandora of opaque delicate mist
There is unusual hope that roads travelled can be paths ended,
With slight overturns and moves across,
Life can be wonderful and sorrowful continuously flowing,
On waters though coarse.

— **Part II** —

Sonnets

Clefs and tones of the musical piece
resoundingly vibrate the entire room
Deep inflections travel in space, across the hollowed deep rows
And by every fret that makes the pervading tune
I find myself waltzing by styled accordions

It felt liberating as I slid through every corner of
    the columned room
Prancing around a tapestry significantly sliced
in portions and bits that build the whole gauntly frame
Couched under slits of the dancing melodic silk

Soft, smooth, and beguiling
Carousing across the bay of eyes that gaze quite sternly
Seas of dismay and flamboyance fleet away
Floating around the peculiarities of my juxtaposed feelings

Yet constantly owning the floor for hours on end
In that train of silky green dress, I've boldly stood
in postures freeing and breathing with sighs and happy cries
There is consonance in flailing sights.

Dazzling Haze

Whatever dazzles in the sullen sordid haze
Untangles the knots of wrought silver chains
In dim-lighted structures of grandiosity
I see someone of a dazzling taste

Taste that leaves you elated wanting for more
Undefinable to the senses, raptures the unknown
And in many dimensions, above layered textures
Of technicolor and contrived rhetoric.

Glaringly, a kind stupor of nobility and poise
Stands by the scaffolding
Encompassing the brightness of the sunlight
A growing composed pallor.

He enters to the threshold of the rouge
And the creases, he beautifully ironed
And all the bronzes and silvers cracked to become gold
Sparkles of fire and gleams of future sights behold.

The Man

Just as a girl I was, I felt a rush of romantic blush;

Across the room, your gaze, your stature and your wondrous
    silhouette threw me in a hush;

No sound, just my heart trying to stay calm

My eyes followed and I whispered: "He's the man".

whose smile glimmered hope in the darkest of nights;

that colored the town with his beaming sight;

that unchained the shackles of fears and doubts;

that untangled the knots of my unsure routes;

And the chimes that go with saying his name, I will never forget,

As it sounds like a lullaby, a melody I have set

And while there he goes, with his princely strides,

It vividly hits as he stopped by my side,

His familiar scent, his manly vibe

I know this time, it's a love I can survive.

Dried Flowers In Old Pages

The excellently written love proses are from you
the grandiosity and emotional vulnerability
hoist my inner thoughts around
I put flowers in these antiquated leaves
to remind me of the scent,
of your high-brazen peculiar verses
that left me awake fixed at the pages.

I put them by the corner
coruscated by twinkling shimmers
of gold dusts and tremendous sparks;
and by the old pages imprinted are the weary dried flowers
yet still as fresh as I remember them to be.

Flushes and blushes
—and inextricably hallowed;
I keep in my rugged memory
that though they wilt and be torn by time
always will be in its prime

Should I?

Should I tell you that the longest hours of my days are
    my thoughts about you?
Should I give my heart the second risk, the mighty frisk of a whip
    that might me hit me back too?
Should I listen to the chaos, to the chords of my tramping heart?
In rhythmic stomps; in breathing cries, as beating pounds
Should I let go of my sorrows and fears that envelope my
    undying dreams?
Should I unlock the doors, and skid my way through
    empty streams?
Should I let my summers turn barren and somber like
    winter freeze?
Of letting go, is there really peace?
Maybe I should, probably I would
Somehow while the raindrop pours, the courage heightens,
    the strength unfolds
That in a bedazzled constellation of stars in colored hues
There is you, and only you.

Your Favorite Song

Inside my down-trodden car,
where everything is messed,
only the stereo plays quite perfectly;
I listen in rounds about the lyrical grace of your favorite song
The impassioned delicacy it emanates
enduringly embracing my shuddering soul.

And the engine revved up, car is geared
the radio continues to buzz scattered tones
But your favorite song plays so clearly
Speaking like elegant ballet moves
Flowing like softly breezed streams.

While on the road, the air kissed my cheeks
And the song still goes on
While remembering your freckled blushed face
Against those hazel doe eyes
That I embarrassingly get lost in trance.

It has become a habit
That every time on the road
It is a sensation of contrived flush and peace
I always play your favorite song.

Just One

Such a lovely lilac aura she possesses
the type of maiden that lads scour through
all over the countries, across oceans terrifyingly deep,
and over streams and ridges askew.
But she belongs to someone else
—do not disturb she and her beau.

Varying degrees of infatuations and enchantments
peppered her bachelorette life
enticing her to grow on fields greener; and
In askance, begged to step on gardens anew.

Engagements that bring forth fresh olives shipped from afar
All packed in line to ask for her
Charmingly decided to present lavish silver-lined oaks
in hopes to win over her
But she loves only one
—in lavender haze
—just one.

— Part III —

By The Vineyard

It's nighttime, the city is wrapped under sheets
The moon lighted my face as I was seated in a sprawled bush
Vines and growing fruits spring like dews
Caressing the sheaths and disintegrated pollens on leaves
And watch them fall to my furling sleeves

The ruffles caught the little petals of the pastel roses
Scent of quick prances, silent breathings, and vanilla concoction
    graze the room
And scuffles I could hear underneath the molasses
Several rumblings of an intrepid grace.

And by the bush hides the wonderful daisies
That bloom in summers, protected in springs
Loved during winters, watched over in autumns
By the vineyard, I watched myself evolve.

Honey And Bees

Yellow and sweet, aboard the sensation of waltzing dews
Dancing like broad leaves, on stacks and hays anew
Fresh buds, delicate and tender
It's the start of summer, a pack of honey and bees out to ponder
—in the world that is enveloped by freezing human palms
—seemingly where to land, where to cradle the produce

In rustic trees, and melodic somber
Honey and bees huddle under
—the nature of greens whilst the scorch and stench
Still in belief of a magnanimous jubilee

And it continues to flow in cycles for years
And though in years there is no deliberate change
—in sighs and pleas to make nature pleasing
For what the honey and bees can joyously bring.

Avalanche

(*Appeared in The Ravens Quoth Press Evermore Anthology*)

Once there was a phantom that frightens during the night
Sneaks through the dimly lit porcelain night-washed light
And by the fireplace, there stood a translucent poltergeist
That mirrors my moves, wrings my hands about, and thrusts
    my sight

Scared but dillydallied with this unfortunate visitor
Sat by the door, importunate and caustic—its lousy
    but egregious humor
Inexorably racked by woes and hoax
It was just me, my reflection in terrible rote.

Avalanche of snowballs and cool freezes
Devoured my entire atmospheric breath
Which goes beyond my callous sorrows
Heaving morosely, succumbing to the ghost.

Ghosts that tremble every night
Gilded by the mourning light
But tomorrows seem to corrode that one maim-flecked instance
In a steep of roundabouts.

Breaking Glasses, Hammering Stoned Houses

The confines of these unbreathable corners make my stomach
    churn
As if it's held by superfluity of freedom about lights
    and crashing burns
—stench of recklessness
Could not afford to climb.

Carefully breaking the glasses in between bricks
    and stones that devour
horrors of all these buried dark streams
Of leaves and soil that envelope the entirety
Every black corner with light impossible to shine through.

Looking from below, it appears like a steeple
About to climb but fall in repetitions, always trying to do so
The stones that press against these glasses that blindingly glimmer
Of gilded patches, yet difficult to break- everything
    remains somber

On breaking ceilings of colored glasses
On hammering out of stoned houses
All begin realities outside thick mists of fantasy
Just as equally hysterical as the inside.

Bad Taste

Distasteful
Displaying luxury amid horrific debacle
Erecting fortresses
For the powerful
Leaving the poor inside rat's squalor

Abhorrent
Carrying onto becoming false kings and queens
Feigned crowns and hinged palaces
Foundation bases on unrecognized labors.

Unforgivable
Poisoning once neat now pale pastures,
Brashly grazed lands,
and patchy rotten soils,
leave a bad taste to national eventual downturns
of old-fashioned perfunctory erosions
uncracked by sealed and tightened collusions.

Sounds Like Mother

Every night, by the windowpane,
cries for a 'mother', lost in an abyss
In reverberating scattered sobs of searching for 'mother',
I burrowed my head, felt inane

Every night, installing my gaslight onto the headboard,
faraway screams of imploring for a figure nestled from a meter
of staggered chatters with heaving chests, begging for 'mother'
I resigned to bed; the sheets furled

Every night, when it was extra thunderous,
There is endless taunting over the window grills,
    seemingly aboard,
in discordant beats and absorbed trembles
Overhearing a writhed noise—'mother'
I must be dreaming, my head rambles.

And tonight, I sat by the glass window
Overlooking the stretch of the bending nature
Growing chorus of 'mother' from the distant end prancing
    towards my direction
The stifling shuffled of dissonant words
I can barely fathom
Mumbles over mumbles, consonants fumble
It was just sounds of dreary dark cats-
My mind is racked.

Maybe If I Were To Cry At Night

I used to believe that keeping myself shut off is the best way
To handle the furies and enameled pains of every day
For it seemingly will not cause havoc or indignation to others
To eschew from naturalness and human platitudes—is that
        the way to go?

But when shutters close,
While inside a thin alleyed corridor, by the dark papered room
I find myself crouching, tugging my thighs on loom
When every soul is fastened in beds,
There I am bawling on end.

Maybe If I were to cry every night, spaces might expand,
Vacuuming from my throbbing chest unhinged
        and splattered bile
To cover the pile of endless heaps of ridges
        and corrugated feelings
To exhale callous winds and fumes so wild,
To pull from the scattered hissings and lowly aptitudes
        —seemingly to expire.

Maybe If I were to theatrically exalt the horrifying
        paroxysms of emotions
Then it would be disastrous to everyone aboard,
While the city resigns come the forlorn nights
Maybe If I were to cry at night, there is solitude despite.

Choked By My Own Flare

I get scolded—
seemingly irritating in the eyes of fellows
I get apprehended—
can do no right to every perfect sight
Quivering in fear, holding on still tight
Endless memories of hatred that propitiously flare

No words ever muttered out—
could not muster the courage
Bellowing rightly so under sheets of covers peppering my soul
By the dust and shame, I truly resemble
Choking on the gigantic parabolas of craze.

I Am Not Insane

I have pondered lately about what you said
It pierced my heart, actively impaled every beating vein
I knew it was injury to my soul but you shrugged
As if it was a terrible slip off, I am not insane.

I have circled my thoughts so thoroughly and quite surely
That every syllabic word was meant to protrude seemingly
Like thick thorns of bushes, scouring to breathe out yielding flares
And spluttered bloods all over, I am not insane.

But stranded voices surround myself
Aghast and appalled—fear envelopes my sanity
Shrouding every inch of me to hide and run away
I know it hurt; I am not insane.

Please, Be Gentle

Onto this journey, I am met with hounds.
It is excruciating to get scorned,
For things I have no grasp about
The mocks and dreary stares devour my conscious being
I can learn. Please, be gentle.

As I go further, I am held by my back
Losing my hold, dropping below
Grimly laughter and caustic blows
I can stand. Please, be gentle.

Borders of a yay and a nay, I hold onto thin strings
About to slip off, yet so tightly I still grip
Puny frame against the Goliaths
I can manage. Please, be gentle.

Deliberate trampling, feigned musings
Apparent shrugs,
On my impotent shrieks
About iterations of doses and pitches
I can. Please, be gentle.

Sense And Sensitivities

Sentience—my superpower
Over a multitude of emotional debacles,
I've learned to be sensible
About circumspections and paroxysms of unapparent dealings
To resurface and take charge of uncarved underpinnings

Words that impale, actions that destroy
Deliberate invalidation of sensitivities, I abhor
Proliferating unsafe spaces,
across unprotected strings of scattered pollens
—that fly about in diffidence
—finding better lands to flourish and freshly commence
yet despite, misunderstandings turn outright devilish
unable to wrap around hostility in creative differences.

Everybody Thinks She's Perfect

Long auburn hair frames her face so impeccably
It swings unhampered by summer tender breeze
She stands like a mannequin pictured for perfection
Gliding down her skin, a train of silk
Her moment, what a gleaming sensation.

When she enters, everybody looks
Stares from up til down, rumors start to accrue
Everybody thinks she's carved out of superior blessings
But nobody knows her real life dealings.

At night, she wallows in despair
Flinging her hands in dissipated energy
Self-degradations devour her whole being
Seems bespectacled by intimidating bellows
Like a scathed dale in spring.

Like a dangling willow, she dances to the beat
Slow and humid. Scared and defeated.
Every time she walks, thorns thrust to her sole
Every time she gives, her hands turn blue and torn.

Yet everybody thinks she's perfect
As how her facade appears to be
Amid frustrations and somber realities
Still, nobody believes.

I Am Alone

In this large mansion, I reside for most of my life
Sprawled by antiquated furniture and paintings
Colored like an enlivened king's pride
From the outside, it dazzles with beaming golden things
But inside bespeaks of horrors and sullen dreams

By this old-fashioned couch, scathed with tiger claws
Huge enough to embrace my fashion hauls
From long dresses to pompous gowns for balls
I'm alone, no sea of crowds, though.

By the endless steeps of a hollowed staircase
That echoes my cries for a humanly grace
Goes about rounds and rounds through the roof
I'm alone, no lines of souls.

By this gigantic bedroom sits all the lavender flowers
By lads of counties and councils afar
Arranged seemingly to welcome a princess aboard
I'm alone, flowers start to wilt away.

But onlookers say I have it all
Who doesn't, anyway, in that aristocratic hole?
Noble and monarchic, they have assembled
But the truth is, I am all alone.

It's Okay Mama!

Two cotton-shaped furs greet me each day
For every good morning,
is a perceptible grin I give back
Words at naught, fumbling sounds simply
But it resonates with definiteness
—all niceties.

When they glare at my emaciated frame,
Two deep-blue peepers pierce my soul
Magnanimous to see through my reckless aches
Like mirrors, they resemble my ruminations
And as I quietly beseech,
assiduously granting their angelic prowess
to my constant derision.

And when they plea,
I am all they have
And for every time I bend to their level
They flung to me
It's okay 'mama'—derived from the high-pitched mumblings
—my cats soothe me, solicitously
—they know, definitely.

Tomorrow If I Die

Tomorrow if I die, please don't cry
I've had long years preceding my death
to have seen you with smiles;
I resolutely demand you to keep your cool
it's enough flagellation
I'm all good.

Tomorrow if I die, no flowers please
I don't want to see them wilt
during unscented springs
Those mean at naught in constant derision
Like how my life has been
terrible apprehensions.

Tomorrow if I die, just leave me bare
That's a cycle after all, I'm done to dare
about how living ought to be
about uncharted sorrowful schemes;
Stories do end
Here, I forebode to thee.

— **Part IV** —

Paralyzed

Colder nights—
oh so divine
like falling mocking jays
hitherto in autumn space.

Shivers and shrills
from across the iced bay
like birds propping
in hasty snowflakes.

Down the spine
pecks of silvers in dosages
Freezing as winter
paralyzed, it seems.

Someone Is Coming

There he is, he came back!
a silhouette I see
from the high fences,
I glared at him trotting towards my home

There he is, I am blithely waiting!
for him to present himself at the door
but it's been hours
the clock hand has stricken past several hours
Where is he? I feel delirious.

Across the expansive meadows,
a shadow showed
but not like him, he is not here
playing with imaginations
my twisted tribulations.

Calm

Impervious by nature—
stands austere, so grand
Thrown at disarrays and mocked for her failings
Hoisted around like spring popinjays
Still remains steadfast,
foot bolted to the ground

Quakes shake her core like perturbed lava flow
Facing situations indulging quite a big stir
Flings around adulterated succor
Still clings on her stoic stupor.

Her calmness penetrates worldly pitfalls
Destructive storms never uproot her rancor
Beyond the upheavals—so exhaustingly
Still breathes without disturbed beatings.

Deliberate Hope Amid Rage And Poignance

Raging salt breeze
Across still, crystal, and rhythmic seas
An untethered tale of delicate warm crease,
There is still bliss;
—for about days and nights of harrowed tides,
On that day forth, resounding waves of glimmer shore rides,
There is unperturbed, unforced peace

Though there is poignance in sordid gentleness
Still dreaming about comfort and bliss amid ineffable feelings
Amid being unhinged by crass emotional dealings

And despite the flailing, the underpinning of the craze
There is the blinding and dancing fire to spark and glare
For futures that hold a glaring and hopeful sight
Bruised by flaws, unhinged by years despite,
Still finding magnificence in melancholic nights.

Locks And Chains

Locks and chained wires suffocate my soul,
Dreaded feelings of despair and hope capture the unknown,
Fears in haze, whiffs of uncertainty,
a pallor countenance, waves of bestiality.

Terrible whispers of dark tomorrows haunt my todays
Telling me sorrows, pain and an importunate hollow space
On loud knocks and eerie screeching sounds of an alluring hate
Stomping on sands, falling ashore and anxiously treading
    in unbeknownst weight

But in the budding of the sunrise, hopes seem to glare
Dancing around the spots of shines and rays just equally bare
Despite my frailty and my corrosive thoughts on days and nights
To breathe under burrows, to capture a future with
    a wonderful sight

Keys to all these wires, all shackled and tightened by the depths
    of beliefs and uptight fights,
To stand taller for magnanimity and presence, hence quite;
Yet musky, unsure, perturbed by quakes and daze
Still rowing towards the endless glimmer for a lingering
    state of grace

December Tides

Salt hair, scruffy skin, there comes the gentle breeze
While wrapped in ivory, the wind blew over that gilded dress
    like it dazzles in a quirky tease
Standing tall, though a bit arched, eyes gaze below the precipice;
And feet tingling by the crestfallen shore crease.
But seemingly though,
I'm still above the stingy lines, with gaze onto the far horizon,
    onto the raging sunlight
And there- right before my glowing might
I see somehow that through great respite,
There is peace on rhythmic December Tides

Strange Little Things

I whispered to the wind while I was seated across the waves,
That all the little things are heavily commensurate
To a poignant fate.
When I got up and slithered my way onto the waters,
It felt like droplets of crystals glided through my sun-dried skin
And walked over with an anxious presentiment,
Yet still proceeded though with clear falters.
Halfway the ocean, I stood there barefoot
Scared but a courageous spirit to soothe
My mind and my heart peacefully playing the beat of tomorrows,
In an endless cycle of rustic melodies.

Sunflowers

Mornings that glimmer thousands of rays,
Lined in unwavering parallels,
Crossed like arrays
Over pompous petals
—that huge focal transfixed;
Breaths of untamed sunshine,
In the moment of rapid faith;
As it grooves to a mirage of elation,
Breezed the scent of acquired sensation
Reels of phantasm hollered
About sunflowers emanating light and warmth
To a dreary heart.

The Swinging Chair

Back and forth, it swings excessively and out of melodies
No rhythms to follow, no sounds onto the tune
And hastily it goes in dissonant beats
Again and again, continuously rocking in ragged feats

Toes spring up, careful not to touch the parquets
Made with exquisite bounds of superfluous grounds
That emanate shines and glitters of gilded brown patches
Back and forth, the lights glide down in harmony
Like singing phantoms in opera day springs

Back and forth, giddily as it goes by quickly
Feels like simplicity of childish activities
Crouched while face down looking below and above
While it rides like undulated coasters in paradise springs
Pictured like wall-colored hues and growing pastel blooms
That realizing in a world of sulkiness and dooms
There lies the rogue of a free spirit and a careless fever
For undaunted adventures- back and forth.

Pepper And Salt

A concoction that creates a multitude of possibilities
Adopting abstract but endless of rationalities
Our minds that border between sense and a bulk of sensibilities
That may outweigh the other- more salt, less pepper please.

Adjunct yet separable- piece by piece our decisions start to weave
Held every so often on dark bricks and hued, wavering crossroads
And in haze and dullness there is an absurd impetus
A thrust that rows across wide range of dart boards.

Perfect taste of that mixture of evergreen and drought
That come forth about calculations of risks and magnitude
A little of that, but sprinkle more of this,
while straddling along rigid routes
More pepper, less salt—this time, a little subdued.

Water In A Bottle

Why should a water be bottled?
To limit its form inside fortifications
To make it still and unmoving
As a calm serenity it purports to bring

How different are the waters in rivers from the waters in glasses?
Thunderous cheers with glasses held up high, or
Cool splashes and stifled waves over green molasses
Across a vast bed of crystalline dancing dews.

As the dew drops to every stenciled stone, to ridges in hills
    or rocks in sore
Or perhaps droplets of water contained- so pure and distilled;
both waters are useful and joyous to serve its purpose
To quench parched lips in unbending ruse
Despite the disparities in creative appropriations
Warranting calls for all worldly situations.

— **Part V** —

From Dusk To Dawn

As preposterous as it may sound, I've waited from dusk to dawn
By this heavy rock, I've pondered completely on
The horizon that flashes right in my vision
Straight to my memories and disillusionments

About worldly pitfalls and enchanting embarkments
About imperfections, peculiarities, and alluring entanglements
Across satiations and perturbed disturbances
I've patiently waited for changes

Traversing a series of steep precipices
Hanging onto wrought handle breaks in every step
Staggers along mountain hills
Breathing heavily, hard sweat spills

That though plaintive in hindsight, and unnatural as snide
Still carrying on forward despite staggering over
    corrugated blocks
Over loose threads stretching to fervid heights
Dawning fecundity and might.

I Know

Of days and nights, I am wrapped in flower patches
Like it's a lullaby sung in safety;
I've grown accustomed to undeterred dandies,
despite corrosive superfluities.

Of springs and summers, I am held under
intrusive blooms sprawled like dancing flakes
And how it taps every corner
from a classic daze
to a pervasive haze.

I know these changes scurry me through
Fiascos of creativity
In trance of peculiarity
Imminence abounds.

She Is A Girl

A lass, a girl, a woman by nature.
Is she really?
But she curses, and she cuts you up but never sutures.
She cries and fumbles and staggers along the roads
That she has traversed and ended magnanimously victorious.

A lass, a girl, a woman by power.
Frightening, isn't she?
She crosses kilometer-deep oceans, jumps from
    a frighteningly high steep
And though she falls like paper neat, still standing tall bare feet.

A lass, a girl, a woman by circumstance
People gaze at her askance
Is she really that tough or is that a creative charade?
That purportedly borders a defiant woman—just so
    scaringly self-made.

She's a lass, a girl, a woman—that is limpid
Remember her peculiarities, her unique diversions,
    and developed prowess
That stir up people's thinking and challenge our arousals
That she's a girl beyond her story—being a woman is her arsenal.

Shaped Droplets

During the mornings, polished as dews
Like blooms by the threshold, they elegantly frame
while coruscated by linear shines of diverse rays
gallant and brave, protruding grace.

Bellowing against the plasters
of honey-freckled sensations;
Grazing and leering, gaily suggesting
echoes of melodic frays.

Droplets unknown
Molded with certainty
Watching them fall on inevitability
Here forth an undying stability.

Take A Sip

A cup of tea stashed with cubes of sugar
For spice and a little bit of figurative taste
The tender sugar beads over a steaming peppermint
Take a sip—it's a summer breeze

A cup of tea poured over with spoonfuls of honey
To blend in color and texture, sweetness enamors
The aroma and flavors evaporate to thin air
Apparent to myself, it's the soothing charm that plasters my fate
Towards the diverse concoction

A cup of tea sits by the cooling pad
As my eyes gather around this expansive cottage
While crickets bowed to the waltzing leaves
The air kissed my sun-freckled skin
Elemental to the riveting senses
Forth to traverse.